The author was born in 1961 in Amman, Jordan, and belongs to an old Jerusalemite Arab family which has been for centuries the custodian of the key of the Church of the Holy Sepulcher. He received his school education in Jordan, Egypt, Italy, Britain, and thereafter was awarded a bachelor's degree in political science from Columbia University and a master's degree in Near Eastern Studies from Princeton University. He possesses an interest in Arabic and English poetry and literature. He worked for a period of time in journalism, and also worked in the public and private sector. For around 20 years now, he has practiced translation as a profession, where he owns a translation office, The Ubada Center for Writing and Translation Services. In general, he has an interest in human thought, irrespective of cultural underpinning.

To all people of goodwill who serve God and strive to make
the world a better place…

Khaled Hazem Nusseibeh

WHY?

AUSTIN MACAULEY PUBLISHERS™
LONDON • CAMBRIDGE • NEW YORK • SHARJAH

ISBN – 9789948347781 – (Paperback)
ISBN – 9789948347811 – (E-Book)

Application Number: MC-10-01-8160961
Age Classification: E

First Published (2020)
AUSTIN MACAULEY PUBLISHERS FZE
Sharjah Publishing City
P.O Box [519201]
Sharjah, UAE
www.austinmacauley.ae
+971 655 95 202

Limitless gratitude and appreciation to my parents and family who have stood by me untiringly over the years. A word of appreciation, however insufficient, to the noble and prodigious Hashemite Prince El Hassan Bin Talal for being a kind human and a beacon of intellectual sophistication. Special thanks to my cousin Zaki Nusseibeh, my splendid uncle Sabih Masri, and Fahim Nusseibeh for their generous support, both moral and material. I am grateful for the guidance and knowledge imparted to me by many, many teachers, friends and mentors who exercised so much influence over me, too many to enumerate.

Introduction

It is "Why", indeed! This is a beautiful, didactic collection of verse that has breadth and substance, questioning our inner being and soul while lifting our spirit to a higher being.

The words are carefully chosen, appealing, immensely creative and powerful to show the delight of the language and how it can be used to deliver very important sets of messages to extrapolate our existence on earth and its relationship to the universe and its creator, the Almighty God.

The author provides rich meanderings of free verse to show the diversity of our universe and its linkage to our region of the world. There is a very powerful message in the individual poems on Gaza, Nablus, and Jerusalem, and an appeal against the abhorrence of occupation and how it wrecks people's lives. Here, the use of words is not harsh but powerfully and masterfully conveyed, stressing the coexistence of the three monotheistic religions of Islam, Christianity, and Judaism.

This book of thought, as Nusseibeh terms it, is an endearing intellectual endeavor and a vivid and impressionistic reflection designed to dwell on poetic justice, aesthetic reverence, and spiritual devotion to a world crafted by the sanctity of the Great, Powerful, Almighty God and His hegemony over the universe. Individual poems dwell on the power of the Almighty God, Islam, the purity of our ablution and prayer, and yearning for what is right and just.

There are powerful words like absolute, veritable, hell-fire, evil, despoiling, wanton killings, and victimization. But these are quickly juxtaposed to righteous deeds, angelic, chants of praises, faith, appeal to the senses, and the cosmic life. And they go down to the exposition of the splendidness of virgin oil, blossoming flowers, and spirit of progress, giving the reader a tour de force of spiritual imagination and the doggedness of modern life.

Dr. Marwan Asmar
Amman, 22/5/2016

The Duke and the House's Lady

A bland, somewhat-busy, and meandering uphill road
Led to the Duke's quaint Amman home
An open gate adorned by pine and cypress trees
Aged and gracefully overarching the space
Atop Jebel Jofeh is perched the dwelling
Overlooking the distant, great Citadel Mountain
As well as the other hills of ancient Philadelphia
Including the riveting Amphitheater of Rome
Traces of bygone ages
And testaments to an unfolding present
Is it a quarry that I eye?
Or a workshop for sculpting marble and stone forms?
The den's entrance is by two steps preceded
Of attractive and solid stone
Is this the den of a collector of art?
Or a patron of the production of culture?
The balcony at the edge of the space is a marvel
Rectangular with two long tables
Three including I sit on dark green chairs
Eying astounded the urban view
Do the ancient hills of great Amman speak
The untold story of epic tales?
Does not each stone silently narrate
The great saga of human settled life and strife?
Or harmony anchored in the will to befriend
To make compassion and love triumph
An electrifying sound grips the scene
As Muezzins from many directions melodiously declare

Allahu Akbar, Allahu Akbar
God is Great, God is Great
The savant in the human encounter impressively relates
Historical stories of the assorted nations and tribes
Can I compare them to sand inexorably blowing in the
wind?
Or water that from heaven pours and then vanishes?
Only to imbue life with recurrent force
Energy that drives life onwards
Harnessed by transient Man
That lives and dies to worship God
The short wall in front of the long table
Holds assorted, old sculptures
And also a bizarre dark brown wooden frame
Including two wooden clogs hanging by thin threads
Delicious lentil soup is gracefully served and consumed
In a tryst that might genuinely be memorable
An Egyptian Copt helps in serving the meal
Alongside the refined and gracious host
The atmosphere is hazy but starkly sunlit
While a weak wind gently blows.
80CR

Long Live Gaza

Like sailing in tremendously stormy seas
In the eye of a terrible gale
Winds that bring untold suffering
To the heroic people of Gaza
Students that study to candle night
And bakers that cannot cater to those in need
Deprived of essentials but not the right to be
To defend, to live, to build a promising future
For children for whom war has become the norm
Youngsters who deserve succor and aid
And elders who spend life's remaining time
Enduring distress, pain and sorrow
Valiance is of epic proportion
Equaled only by the inaction of brethren abroad
Scores of states that do not lift a finger
To alleviate untold human suffering
Must our next of kin dig perilously deep into the earth
By dint of iniquitous closures?
Must dialysis machines receive only a meager ration
Of electricity to sustain fragile life?
And yes, O Israel, can you not awaken
To the reality of a history of inordinate suffering
Only to become projected on defenseless folk
Whose only sin is the will to live, to build, and to endure
Steadfastness that is of truly rare parallel
Inscribing Gaza's blood, tears and sweat on history's great
saga.
৪৩

Remembering the Islamic Liberation of Jerusalem

A memory as sweet as honey can be
Salah Eddin's monumental feat of liberation
The sacred soil tells a sad tale
Of estrangement, prolonged and grievous
The golden dome has great luster
Dimmed by the occupation's sordid reality
God is Great resonates
The cathedral's bells toll
Repeatedly, painfully, loudly
But the resonance is to date abortive
Jerusalem- beloved in heaven and on earth
Shall I compare you to a priceless gem?
Coveted profoundly but insufficiently valued
Like the sun that emits warm and golden rays
Happy are those that nurtured its hallowed soil
And honored the covenant to worship Him alone
Leaving no stone unturned to safeguard the dwelling
To anchor the tired hands in a fragile living
Ominous has destiny become
Injustice tearing away at living's fabric
Alas Al-Quds is a city of veritable peace
To be erected by solemn prayer and determined action
The will to overcome the penchant to usurp
To twist the truth for worldly gain
Somehow, men and women of faith, dawn shall break
And redemption and salvation shall come to pass
However deep the well
Whatever the extent of suffering

Within the ambit of cosmic life
The angels venerate the Great Lord
And the humans keep chanting the praise of God
That triumph overwhelms sinister defeatism
And evil is vanquished by righteous deed
Anchored in a human chain of faith and sense.

ജ‌ൠ

Our Mother Nablus

Etched in the vast recorded history
Is the great mountain of fire
Doesn't the mountain of Jerzim shed tears
That its neighbor Ebal is likewise in chains?
Shekem reveals many a chapter
Of an indomitable will to be
To survive in dignity and freedom
To keep the minaret chanting God is Great
And the cathedrals remember the hermits of old
That lived to venerate the Lord
Flavius the Roman constructed the new city
A valiant Neapolis that is as old as time
Menaced by multitudes of invading forces
Wreaking havoc, despoiling the green land
Of the numerous surrounding hamlets
Embodying a dazzling history, and a glorious present
Of people who steadfastly endured
And nurtured a splendid living tradition
Do the Samaritans yearningly bemoan
The eclipse of the great Umar
And the twilight of a magnificent civilization
That radiated a culture of justice and dignified living?
If only the orphaned city can tell
The repressed wounds of prolonged occupation
And the terrible scourge of indifference
By a nation spread throughout the globe
The wall of Jacob, the tomb of Joseph
A saga of immense tribulation and vindication
To light the flames of pure and virgin olive oil
And to cleanse impurity with the finest soap

Beloved mother, Arab city of Nablus
We bow with sincere reverence at your epic tale
That tells a history of steadfastness without parallel
In the face of the great vicissitudes of time
The Kassaba will once again be illumined
With lanterns fueled by the blessed oil
And the two sad mountains will rejoice
That the time of liberty has drawn nigh.

୫୬

A Time for Faith

I roam the earth wandering
In quest for my passionate love
The time has drawn nigh, O Lord
For life's essential moment
When there is flight from terrible sin
And a return to the Great God
A moment of sanctity
A time of faith
An hour to mark the veneration of God
To worship Him without partner
Let's tread the path of the believing souls
Who walked the alleys of reason
Isn't He life's quintessential element?
Pre-eternal, Omnipotent, Omniscient, Merciful
I yearn for Your unimaginable love
I seek the Truth of Your eternal Being
Transcending finitude
Defying evanescence
A solitary soul searching for rational proof
Only to fathom a vast cosmos
In which is manifested His eternal Glory
Where I stand lesser than a drop of rain
Or a vanishing dark shadow
Or a passing sweet wind
The heart doubts O Lord
Amid unassailable certitude
Hovering over all of existence
Preserving life, nurturing truth
I find You in Your Glorious epiphany
In your uncreated Qur'anic speech

Transporting me from a feeble sea wave
From a limping walk
From a tiny amount of evaporating water
From a veritable finitude
To a riveting apprehension
A stunning perception
Of an <u>Unseeable</u> Master
Of an immense cosmos
Let the devils not fool you
Let the flickering stars not mislead you
Life is a moving mirage
Of preordained pain or veritable joy
I seek You in the depth of my heart
In the induction of my mind
In the world of mammals
In the splendid existence of plants
I know that I am
And recognize that You know
I, an illusory sparkle of a distant planet
And You, the sole Creator of all.

ℰↄ♋

Why?

When all is said and done
The dust settles
The clouds move in the sky
The noise of children abounds
Has the crisis abated?
Do we have naught to tell?
If only I could describe
And accurately gage
The twinkling of a star
The crest of a wave
The splendid shining of the moon
Why is blood's color red?
And why is the skin's color dark?
How do earthly satellites orbit?
The inquiries are troublesome
To the savants of the age
On the edges of life live
The beings of the latter day
To be witnessed, observed, and seen
For the questions are immensely more
Than the answers embodied in elusive and fragile life
The darkness is penetrated by flickering lights
Glimmers issuing like unfathomable ghosts
Can I touch the rays of the sun?
The matter is beyond reason's bounds.
ഇരു

Let's Sing the Praises of God

The mind is boggled by the idea
Life's both enduring and ephemeral four seasons
Is the winter of our discontents upon us?
Or does the autumn of fury await us?
Every season ineluctably moves on
Only to leave behind a bitter and sweet harvest
Even the spring of fertility and fecundity lapses
Immense regeneration succeeded by bewildering aridity
The fast-moving seasons perennially outlive the human
Does it matter in which season a human departs?
Nature is endowed with tremendous staying power
Itself subject to decay and renewal
The flowers blossom beautifully in the time of spring
Adorning nature's green and lush terrain
Verdant hills, mountains and plains
Embracing the beguiling illusion of permanence
Can Arabs fathom the illusoriness of spring?
Or must Persians catalyze protest?
Reformation that is as essential as water and air
To humanize and rationalize a declined society
A community in need of the spirit of progress
The impulse for self-cleansing and purification
A reaffirmation of the cardinal principles of equality
Of faith, liberty, justice, and advancement
Never in the annals of human history
Has so much been sacrificed for the narrow interests of the
few
The immense landscape of history attests
That this nation was born for greatness
To illumine humanity's path

To be witness to the human community's rectitude and folly
To light ablaze the torches of freedom
To emancipate those everywhere in chains
To edify the world in the supreme value of monotheism
Wedded to a vision for a better life for all
To be achieved even if by lighting small candles
By removing dirt from the path of pedestrians
Or vastly more importantly
By engraving "God is Great" on every aspect of life
So is the way forward, fellow men and women
Let us behold the moment of sanctity
And unwaveringly witness that God is One
Without partner or coequal
The Lord who created existence in its entirety
Without need for succor or help
Let's move away from perdition's sinister path
And join in unison to sing the praises of God.

෫ාකා

A Bunch of Grapes

A tortuous journey drew nigh
Feet bloodied, garments torn
The blessed Muhammad called them to Islam
The people of the distinguished city of Taif
Addas the Nazarene encountered him
With an offering of a bunch of grapes
A Christian from Nineveh who recognized
The noble prophet of Arabia
Is it not time for the mighty to offer
A bunch of grapes to the earth's wretched?
An emblem of harmony, between rich and poor
Between the powerful and the disinherited
The slum dwellers of Latin America
The children of Shatila and Al-Shate'
Those ailing without treatment
And those hungry without sufficient food
Those deprived of an opportunity
For education, for better health, for better housing
Muhammad was no advocate of sinister rancor
Of hatred driving the quest to be better
Islam, a message of love, peace and harmony
That unites diversity in submission to God.

৪৩

On the Threshold

On the threshold of a new year we stand
Lamenting cascades of blood, untold suffering
As though tormented by unspeakable pain
Diaspora, wanton killing, fratricidal conflict
A region engulfed by the fires of combat
Tribes and nations against each other
Refraining from seeking the peace of nations
Which ought to be anchored in justice and truth
Where the dispossessed deserve redemption of rights
The hungry and the downtrodden a better world, a better life
It is bewildering the extent of malicious actions
Attested to by burgeoning camps, multitudes of refugees
Asylum seekers alienated from their homes, hamlets, cities
Now covered by the debris caused by indiscriminate
bombardment
Has Man lost his soul
Succumbing to the penchant for pugnacity, for hateful
action?
The game of nations has lost its way
Playing by rules neglectful of the victims
Can we in unison dream of an hour of peace
Rooted in a transformed human psyche, a reformed soul?
Yes, powers determined to right what is wrong
By action that converts misdeeds into righteous feats
So that we all mark a time when humanity found its way
On the footsteps of the Adam family- repentant, believing,
and righteous
Rejoice, son and daughter of Adam, the hour may have
struck
When swords are turned into plowshares

For the alternative is much too sordid
Too insufferable, too terrible
Let us together praise the God Almighty
Verily, none but He eternally exists
Naught but He is everlastingly glorified, in heaven and on
earth
The One, Almighty, the Compassionate, the Merciful
From Him we originate, and to Him we shall return.
ჵჩ

Mountain

A seeker of truth is like one
Who slowly climbs and beholds a mountain
Viewing that is of limited perspective
Moving, though, enables wider perception
The other side of the mountain
Is verily not within vision's angle
But feeling, seeing, hearing, and smelling
Enable greater and increasing knowledge
The mountain truly undergoes constant change
The soil with rain turns into mud
And the force of water erodes the rocks
Forming ever-changing configurations
The view of the mountain is quasi infinite
From the top what is seen is small
While proximity to view objects
Engenders more realistic perception
Of size, texture, color, and substance
And all that matter is constituted of
At times the clouds touch the mountain heights
Which is moving, the clouds or the mountain?
Is the mountain solitary or
Is it a part of a range, a constellation?
A material formation punctuating a terrain
To be contrasted with a coastal plain
Mountains convey what is mighty in nature
Awesome towers in our splendid planet
Containing roots that stabilize the earth
Preventing quakes and other calamities
As though anchors of sailing ships
That wish to dock at a safe port

On a wild journey in an unfathomable wilderness
Navigation with imperfect knowledge, effort, and technique
There is in existence a vortex
A solid unshakable rock to anchor at
To build life climbing a mighty mountain
Declaring La Ilaha Illallah
And placing the imperfect matrix
In an equation of infallible belief.

৪৩

Let Us Submit to God

As though shining pearls that dazzle
Pure water washing the bodily parts
An intent to worship the One God
Preceding a great ordained ritual
Beautiful actions that connect
A sinful soul with the Almighty God
A face washed of its impurities
Of sins, of acts of transgression
A visage cleansed of all evil
Prepared for sincere prostration to the Lord
The water is likewise applied
To the two hands up to the elbow
Will only these simple acts please
The Great Deity of Endless mercy?
And water on the back and front
Of the hair of a transgressing soul
Thank you, Lord, for your Commands
A prelude to blessed salvation
Then cleaning the two feet with water
Legs that have trodden sinful paths
Testimony that God is One
And that Muhammad is His Messenger
Then performing blessed prayer
O Lord! Do not expel us from Your Mercy
All praise is due to Him
Who has made so easy the path to surrender
To the valley of good and mercy we must walk
Bearing the weight of untold trespassing
Help us Lord on our paths of tribulation
That we gain your unending favor

To Him we shall return bearing
The burdens of inordinately evil deeds
Accept from us the righteous actions done
At your behest, and with your guidance.
૪૭૪

Columns

No, I do not fail to notice
The lapidary structures of Jerash
Superbly built stone columns
Embellishing the landscape of an old city
Containing theatres, markets, and paved roads
Testament to a great, defunct civilization
Embedded in the Jordanian terrain
Grafted onto an impressive natural environment
Builders who immortalized their deeds
Artists who produced with aesthetic brilliance
Virtuosity captivating the human senses
Dazzling creations of people perpetually seeking excellence
Architectural feats that met the highest standards
Engineering cisterns, aqueducts, roads surviving for
millennia
A city whose vestiges powerfully remind us
That worldly greatness is but an ephemeral, passing
moment.
৪৩

Mutual Denunciation

An irony of monumental proportion is manifest
In the devil's speech in ultimate eschatological time
He taunts his followers for obeying him
And likewise dissociates himself from them
In the world he promised them illusory things
Tempting them to commit evil and unbelief
Bearing toward them an eternal grudge
Owing to God favoring humans over him
His sin of pride drove him to disobey the Lord
Incessantly trying to imbue humans with the same sin
Driving people to contravene Divine injunction
While himself recognizing what is true and false
He well knows the meaning of history's drama
Mystifying and confusing its teleological content
His perennial aim is to lead astray
The most numerous multitudes possible
Humans he will encounter in hellfire
When he speaks to them with foretold astounding irony.

৪৩

Train Station

In a morose mood can I compare you, O life
To a train station bustling with movement?
People in throngs entering and exiting
Boarding and descending from numerous trains
Myriad destinations and multiple directions
As though a metaphor for life's infinite variety
The train of life is boarded
On a wondrous voyage of turbulent, uncertain existence
Beatitude, sadness, and joy encountered on the way
Fraught with the senseless and meaningful alike
An inescapable amount of
Both happiness and grief
Engendered by dint of personal volition
And inaction- or action- committed
The train moves in meandering pathways
Fertile and desert land on its way
Consuming energy for human benefit
People commanding its diverse trajectories
Like stars orbiting in the vast galaxies
Constellations of celestial bodies
God did not permit us a say in the origin of life
For He determines the purpose of all
And did not seek the help of humans in creation's act
A deed of mercy in His immense universe
If only they believe, if only they listen, if only they respond
To his call that He alone be worshipped
That His Legislative Will be obeyed
That His Religion be followed
For all I have savored and experienced of this life
I choose to tread Heaven's Way

And though the self whispers the evil of doubt
Faith is the fruit of human choice and God's guidance alike.
ౠ

33

The Soft Touch of Endless Love

Like the sweet rain that softly touches the earth
Giving life its essential provision
Like the red roses that adorn a landscape
And the daffodils embellishing the fertile terrain
I am at a loss for words to adequately describe my love
A stark white cloud that with fecundity animates life
A coming of souls that is a splendid embrace
Of two people enamored of each other
Like the grass clothing the expansive meadows
Giving vision a noble and invaluable perspective
Or a masterful portrait of lush color and towering virtuosity
Capturing the mighty force of human passion
You are a garden of stunning beauty
Or an orchard of magnificent grace
Driving me to love, to adore, to honor
A bond of forceful and lasting passion
Yes, I will compare you to a distant and wondrous horizon
That touches gently my every sense
And enshrouds the rough edges of a turbulent life
With the soft touch of endless love.

෫෮

Conflict

Conflict has so permeated human history
Punctuating both the dark and bright episodes of time
Systems of ideas propelled actions
Undergirded by both love and aversion
Antipathy to a race forming an ideology
Heterodox in its ideational parameters
White supremacism or negritude
Excluding the other from civilized orbit
Or extremist ideas challenging an urban order
Notions intermeshed with a quest for a changed reality
Or class conflict driven blindly
By a monocausal focus on matter
Or epistemic idealism glorifying a race
Where it is 'proper' that all are its servants
Verily history is underpinned by ceaseless social motion
And movement punctuating inexorably changing fortune
Of individuals, races, classes, and nations
Striving to survive in oftentimes unfriendly environments
Sometimes to expand, at others to retrench
Seeking security, prosperity and oftentimes elusive peace
In the vast oceans of human history
Have been the great torchbearers of truth
Those that affirmed the necessities of civil living
While affirming Islam's timeless creed
For truly the present life is a tiny distance
Incomparable with the infinite voyage of eschatological
time.
৪০০৪

Grievance

Oftentimes he and she that suffer
Strive to understand the cause of grievance
Victimization by men, women, a race, classes
Or the age, or illness, or cultural or economic influence
Thinkers articulate an idiom of protest
Oftentimes monocausally demonizing an aspect
And so, grievances are intellectually addressed
With an ideology that imperfectly comprehends
Thereby unfairly treating a race, a gender, a class, a faith
The "other" that is not within a set of identities
People can overcome by slowly climbing
A mountain of more objective truth
Rendering reality with more circumspection
Removing or assigning blame with balance.
ఇఆ

Longing

The inexpressible joy that I have felt
The pain that withered away
In the deep darkness
Of a summer night
Only to redefine what I have fathomed
In a profound sea of doubt
Overcoming a skeptical self
Unawakened to the truth I sense
In the innermost soul
The deeper regions of the unconscious
Kindle the fire of faith!
And make it ablaze with certitude!
I am not a being at the edge of the universe
Or at its unfathomable center
I yearn for your sincere love
And the unbridled emotion of unending longing
To be enshrouded with a broken will
That staggers in a vast expanse
Submitting to Him who forever is
For I am naught but a passing shadow
A traveler by night and day
Illumined by vanishing stars
Searching within and finding
That all but He is an illusionary flicker
Of veritable truth
Which defies the forces of evanescence
That have been with us all
Since time's earliest dawn
Until the twilight of every day
Of every age, of every epoch

Help me, O Lord, with your speedy succor
That I breathe the rhythms of endless love
Actualized in an unknowable configuration of time
And space in which I cannot travel
I am, O Lord, a slowly moving wave
That strives to reach a near or distant coast
Of fine sand on which I shed my tears
Of exhausting journey
Seeking a sojourn of true love
Not betrayed by the chicaneries of life
The alleyways that have been endlessly trodden
By Man, who insistently does not learn
To be within an orbiting moon
Of true light and unimpeachable truth
Which I strive to apprehend
With hands bound behind my back
In the prison cell of the finite universe
Inexorably expanded by the Omnipotent Creator
Let there be a sound to awaken me
From the slumber of false love
From the cesspool of adulterated perfume
That discharges foul scent
Concealed by a cover of dazzling roses
With sharp thorns producing immense pain
Redeeming those that restore
The right steps of love's authentic dance
Emitting the sweetest aromas
Of the noble Arabian nights
The desert lands in which have dwelled
The soldiers of Mehmet's knights
The monks who shook the core of darkness
Riding handsome white stallions
Doing battle against an inner yearning
To throw an anchor on faith's port
A whitened road
A blackened hill
An immense mountain
At whose heights are perched homes and birds

Overlooking vast plains
Of verdant and fertile terrain
The horizons of hate are brimming
With a quest to deflower purity
To somehow create black tulips
To make the rivulets flow with red blood
And the black ink that darkened
The great and ancient Euphrates
And made vanish the innumerable pages
Composed by intrepid, though succumbing scholars
Men and women that lit endless candles
Red, white, green and blue
Chromatic configurations as varied
As the color shades of clay
From which the Lord created
The family that is the human race
I long for an unshakable rock
To shed the attires of life
To build a mind that I know
Could not abandon its love
For all the boats in the harbor
And all the colorful masts that they bear
Those that circumnavigated the wide earth
Sailing around the cape of good hope
But true hope is rekindled
When the Arabian Ahmad is followed
A mercy to all the worlds
To all the isles, to all the continents
The loving cry of Bilal
The eternal truth of God is Great
The plaintive cry that issued from
An Abyssinian free slave
Converting chains into indomitable
Tools of great liberation
The inner yearnings of souls
Incarcerated by the jails of illicit desires
Indulged only to arouse
An appetite for unfulfilled desire

I seek the song of whole harmony
Green grass that hosts lovely daffodils
Highlands that love in prostration
Preparing a tryst with kind destiny
Male and female dancing to a great tune
A ballad at peace with itself
Ire overcome by true compassion
Bravery that defies the sinister impulses of race
The fables of old have been retold
Beware of evil's folk
The terms of war or peace are defined
The veiled lady is our foe
The minaret produces alien sound
The place of worship is against our kind
The bearded men are hostile
To an old way of life
Our neighborhood must be free
From a system of total truth.
෨൭

Hyperbole

An advancement of human culture
When language precisely describes reality
Objective reality reified
In narratives that accurately portray
Discourses that are firmly anchored
In intellectual activity that empirically observes
Facts, events, phenomena
Recorded in guarded, carefully crafted language
Science and the discourses of the humanities
Circumspectly erecting structures of knowledge
Subjecting the knowable to inductive reasoning
And deducing theoretical postulates
Fusing the visible with metaphysics
By God, the earth around the sun revolves
Plant, animal, and physical reality
Ontologically dependent on the Divine
Poetry, though should not be banished
Nor hyperbole, not superlatives, nor far-fetched metaphor
For language accommodates a vast system of meaning
Containing the potential for infinite variety
My Lord, I wish to catch the moon of life
And relish its lustrous shine
And orbit in the region of its movement
To become the son of the age of space.

ജരു

Thinking

The irrational oftentimes animates human action
Confusedly ascribing effects to erroneous causes
Thinking that the ultimate cause of a condition
Is a particular contingent reason
A political circumstance completely engendered
By a man, a trend, or an extraneous variable
Surely, permeating the landscape of events
Are innumerable causes and influences
Sound reason dictates gaging such multiplicity
While ascribing all to a unitary Originator
Even the basest of evil is not ontologically
Independent from the Ultimate cause of phenomena
Monotheism is perfectly harmonious
With reason and senses that unveil reality
While monotheistic Reality is a supreme truth
Mind and senses vehicle incomplete knowledge.

We Will Overcome

Is it not a pernicious application of "justice"
That the village of Ni'lin should be so abused?
The crime is to resist land expropriation
And the building of an apartheid wall
Dividing a brave little hamlet
Defiant in the face of iniquitous occupation
Olive groves that have been possessed for centuries
Planted and nurtured to sustain a livelihood
Presently threatened by a vicious penchant to seize
To transfigure, to colonize, to violently pacify
Ni'lin, however, is a citadel of steadfastness
Bolstered by activist conscientious objectors
Brave Jews and foreigners who have joined a righteous
cause
To defend a village fighting for its integrity, its survival
For its place in the midst of immense power
That dictates profoundly unfair terms
That treats the victim as an oppressor
And subjects the oppressed to untold suffering
The separation wall will not overcome
A nation's indomitable will to eventually prevail
In God Almighty we place our faith
That a just cause will be redeemed.

છાૹ

Presumption of Innocence

Can we imagine a tightly closed cell opening
Setting free a long-incarcerated human
For too long living in darkness
Counting the days of a fast-moving life
Each day the dread of heavy chains
Inextricably tying an innocent man
Wrongly condemned for a heinous crime
That he is indubitably innocent of
Lamentably, injustice has with justice coexisted
Rendering any system of justice fallible
For no judge but God is omniscient
Nor any jury unfailingly true
Hence, many a time in the history of Man
The culpable were free, the innocent punished
Fortunately, the human justice system has oftentimes
Condemned those guilty of crime
Punishment assures life to society
In the shadow of just laws and fair judgment.
ଛ୬ଓଽ

Loaf of Bread

৪৩

Sorrow at times visits the heart
One observing the unconscionable albeit preventable
A small child inquired about his condition
Initially nodding, but then shedding tears of grief
You know, bread amid fratricidal war is lacking
The elderly and young deprived of sustenance
Not red meat, nor sumptuous food
But a loaf of bread to allay the aching belly
Salvaging the situation is merely a tiny step for many
Immensely insignificant for some, but a matter of basic
survival for others
Perhaps war has visited pain on many a villain
On some culpable of vile crime
But the child starving is utterly blame free
Entirely guiltless and innocent
May a small candle light be lit
To illumine the path of a child in his early years of
tribulation.
৪৩

Harmonious Colors

Verily, human attitudes can radically change
Colors thought dissonant may be viewed as harmonious
The notion of inveterate chromatic antithesis is spurious
For black and white are convergent
Is brown and blue conflictual
Forming a fundamental antithesis?
Observation of vast nature indicates
That immense visual variety is a reality
Diverse color of skin, plants, flowers, and all matter
Is wondrously evident in vast creation
Let us fellow man, celebrate such variety
In its immensity indicative of a Unique God
Unchanging Himself, but embedding the cosmos
With an underlying and all-pervasive law of change.
ೞ೦ಚ

Port of Mercy

47

There's what is astonishing in digits and letters
In combination the possibilities are infinite
Ponder the email configurations
Endlessly formable
Limitlessly configurable
Can two parallel lines intersect in infinity
And are there ultimate boundaries to word construction?
Verbal sculpture is mind-boggling
As though an indomitable, unstoppable quest
An ever-expanding lexicon that is civilization's receptacle
The patent truth is that the two parallel lines
Of both belief and unbelief shall meet
And concur in eschatological domain
Paradise everlasting for the believers
And hellfire eternal for the unbelievers
May one choose the line leading to salvation
And vehicle the approach to safe anchorage
The merciful port of Muhammad
The ultimate truth of Divine Unity.

ॐ

Human Choice

Two approaches to understanding history
One that emphasizes the role of heroes
In animating dynamic movement and progress
Witness the prodigious Toynbee and Carlyle
The other is dialectical materialism
That history progresses irrespective of the creative individual
Historical stages linked to the mode of production
Feudalism, capitalism and proletarian dictatorship
Classless society that ends history
But isn't human choice oftentimes crucial
Moving people to form their reality?
೮つ೮ಚ

Whither Humanity

Subject of debate in every society
The limits of polyphonic reality
Thinkers and sages alike recognize
The vital importance of internal harmony
Some have postulated that pluralism is the end
That each view, every position, is as valid as the other
The debate is multi-disciplinary
With a powerful echo in every field of study
Oftentimes, dissent has awakened nations
Voicing morally imperative views
The evils of racism, the perniciousness of decadence
The Theaetetus succinctly captured the essence of the
debates
Within the monument of the theory of knowledge
How can we validate a proposition?
How do we verify reliably that a perception is true?
Descartes and Ghazali concurred on doubting as an
epistemic vortex
Building systems of ideas that include the central idea
That we live in a universe with a Creator
Wither, it may be asked, is human civilization?
It is arguable that survival hinges inextricably on faith
And a restoration of some norms and values erroneously
discarded
In favor of unbridled materialism, and moral relativism
Leaving humanity alienated from its essence, its purpose, its
trajectory
As the vicegerents of God on earth.

ഇൗ

Now is the Time

What has been done, can't be undone
But now is the time to do what must be done
Awaken fellow man, fellow woman
Let's light the torch of faith
Cry God is Great with a repentant heart
With contrition at things past
Never mind the blackness of the night
Or the stench of the sins done
Kindle a candle of hope bright
Illumining the dark corners of a life spent
Praise the One who created dark and light
And choose to be among those that do right
A heart's glance at the Almighty God
And a few ounces of water to wash
A proclamation that there is Only One God
And that Muhammad is the Messenger of God
Believe this tired soul, this is the right path
To everlasting bliss and unending paradise
And avoidance of an endless abode in the fire of hell.

ॐ